Joseph

Olwyn Harris

Reflections on a Reflections on a boy who grew
through rejection to be a person of influence

Suitable for Individual and Group Discussion

Copyright © Olwyn Harris 2025

ISBN Softcover   978-1-923021-46-4
      eBook   978-1-923021-47-1

All rights reserved. No part of this book may be reproduced or transmitted in any form or by any means, electronic, or mechanical, including photocopying, recording or by any information storage and retrieval system without the permission in writing by the copyright owner.

Unless otherwise stated Scriptures quoted here are from the King James Version (Authorised version). First published in 1611. Quoted from the KJV Classic Reference Bible, copyright 1983 by the Zondervan Corporation.

Published by: Reading Stones Publishing
Helen Brown & Wendy Wood
Woodwendy1982.wixsite.com/readingstones
Cover Design: Olwyn Harris. Some of the cover elements were created using AI Technology.

For more copies contact the publisher at:
Glenburnie
212 Glenburnie Road
ROB ROY NSW 2360
Mobile: 0422 577 663
Email: Readingstonespublishing@gmail.com

Acknowledgement:

My heartfelt appreciation to Pastor Dawn Peel, emeritus, who has held a role as part of the credentialing of pastors within the ACC church. Thank you for your willingness to cast your theological eye over these chapters.

Table of Contents

Joseph

Table of Contents ___ 5
Introduction ___ 7
Ridges and Troughs ___ 9
The Trough of Slavery ___ 20
The Ridge of Stewardship ___ 30
The Trough of Suffering ___ 44
The Ridge of Service ___ 58
The Trough of Suspicion ___ 68
The Ridge of Sonship ___ 79
Appendix: Offering and Seeking Forgiveness ___ 93
Endnotes ___ 96

Introduction

Taking time to reflect on the stories in the Bible, is something that we are encouraged to do in our walk with Jesus. I don't know anyone who would suggest this is not an important aspect of being a disciple of Jesus. Yet I have noticed, over and over, there is a widespread illiteracy regarding the stories in the Bible which I grew up with. I've also noticed that this unfamiliarity is not restricted to new Christians. I suspect we are more comfortable with the popular narratives on our TV streaming service, than the ones in our Bible.

The Holy Spirit, in his wisdom, has chosen the platform of storytelling as one way to communicate our spiritual relationship him, packed with wisdom, truth, morality, and values. It is not the only way God speaks to us, yet so much practical wisdom can be distilled from these narratives. Our challenge is how to access these stories in a way that allows them to be understandable in a world that is so far removed from the times when these accounts occurred. This series on *Reflections in the Bible* is not intended to be an exercise in theological exegesis, rather to create an opportunity to explore some of these stories. It is an invitation to go on a journey of reflection around what is described. What can we distil from these life-stories that makes sense for us today? Some of these narratives may be familiar. Some of them may be forgotten. Some of them are hard to understand. This is an opportunity to take time to slow down, invite the Holy Spirit to whisper his insight as we explore some of the stories he has preserved for us.

This book is intended to be a reflective space to use alongside your Bible. Sometimes, even the act of opening the pages of our Bible can be a challenge. So, open up! Don't skip over the suggested passages marked as "Bible Readings". The scriptures tagged as "Bible

Reference" are intended to bookmark passages, if you want to check them. Take hold of the opportunity to read or revisit God's Word. You are invited to use these pages as a place to scribble in margins; explore your own questions; and use reflective prompts to go a little deeper. My prayer is that it will be a springboard to explore the incredible love story of God, his great good news of redemption and His grace will draw you closer to who He is as our Good Father. I trust it moves each of us to appreciate more about our relationship with God, ourselves and life in community.

1.

Ridges and Troughs

As I was considering the life of Joseph in the Old Testament, it became clear to me that Joseph's life was a life of ridges and troughs. High places and low places. Yet we see that both these places, the highs and the lows, were not dependent on his success as a person. Rather it was his connectedness to God that we notice was defined as his success.

One day I was praying with a lady, and as she was praying, she received a prophetic picture from the Holy Spirit. I was unemployed at the time, and she told me that God had shown her a warehouse - she couldn't see what was on the door, or the name of it, but as I walked past this warehouse, the door opened, and God would give me a job there. Then she said, that although I might not feel I was able to do such a job, God wanted me to know that I was the right person for the job for that season, that I could do this job and that God has positioned me there. This word was so exciting for me! So, encouraging. God saw me and I was getting a job!

Sometimes life is like that, doors opening, opportunities coming at us. We can feel like we are riding a wave, things are moving fast, it seems life is working well, and we are getting wins. But sometimes the reverse is also true of our experience. Sometimes, just as quickly it seems we can hit a trough. Things are hard, like ploughing through mud, being sucked down, trying to make headway and not quite making it.

The picture that comes to mind as I think about this is the ridges and the troughs in the sand at the beach. Sometimes we are walking along a ridge, enjoying the surf and the water and life is good!

Where have I considered my experience of living on the ridge – as evidence that I am doing everything right?

Then sometimes we can feel the bottom drop out from underneath us and we find ourselves in a trough that has a strong rip. And life suddenly turns to struggle, and we can feel like we are drowning, and it doesn't seem that we did anything to make it change, except trying to move forward. But it has changed. Very much.

Where have I considered my experience of struggling in a trough – as evidence that I am doing everything wrong?

How could I support myself to be more objective in assessing what is happening?

The question I was asking myself as I thought about this was: are the troughs in life inevitably part of our story? Or should we be fighting the troughs? Should we be trying to flatten out the landscape? Should we be trying to navigate life in a way so that we stick to the ridges?

So, as we start these reflections on this great hero in the Old Testament Joseph, son of Jacob, we are going to explore it through this lens of ridges and troughs, to see a bit more of how we can be encouraged as we encounter our own ridges and troughs in life. Let's look at the account in Genesis 37 where the account of Joseph is drawn into focus.

Bible Reading
Genesis 37:1- 4

Jacob has issues

So, the back story to this account is that Jacob, Joseph's father, is Abraham's grandson. Jacob escaped the anger of his twin-brother Esau, when he cheated him out of his birthright, and went to live with his uncle Laban, on his mother's side. Joseph's father Jacob had issues, no doubt about it. Yet God is present in his story.

Jacob falls in love with Laban's daughter, Rachel and contracted with his uncle to work for Rachel's hand in marriage by working seven years. Laban however, substituted Rachel's older sister (Leah) on the wedding night so Jacob ended up married to Leah instead. Jacob married Rachel as well, by agreeing to work for another seven years. He loves Rachel and tolerates Leah, which is a great family dynamic to be part of. So, Jacob is married to both sisters, but all is not happy in the house of Jacob.

Rachel has issues

Joseph's mother Rachel had issues, no doubt about it. Yet God is present in her story. We read that there is intense rivalry between the sisters. Leah doesn't like Rachel, because she is loved by Jacob and she is not. Rachel is jealous of Leah, because Leah has been able to have six children, and she has not been able to get pregnant at all.

There were all sorts of trades that the sisters made, to keep the upper hand in this family competition. One example is that Leah sold some mandrake root to Rachel (used to induce fertility), if Rachel would agree Leah could have a night with her husband. Then Rachel used her maid Bilhah as a surrogate, a normal cultural practice, and in that way had children through her handmaiden. Leah does the same thing with her maid Zilpah. So now Jacob has a large family of ten sons and at least one daughter is named in scripture.

Then, in Jacob's old age, Rachel falls pregnant. She gives birth to Joseph which means "Jehovah increases". Rachel's greatest desire is fulfilled. She falls pregnant again and this time, she dies in childbirth, giving birth to Benjamin. Rachel is buried in Bethlehem.

It is a saga of jealousy and conflict, hardly the picture of a godly household and peaceful family that one would expect from a patriarch of God's chosen nation. But now that Rachel has died, it doesn't get better.

Have I have taken my parent's issues to mean that this somehow disqualifies me from experiencing God's goodness in my life?

Joseph has issues

Jacob dotes on Joseph and indulges him. He was his first son born to the love of his life, Rachel. And the way I read it is that Joseph grows up as a spoilt brat. He's a dobber and a tittle-tat, bringing bad reports back to his father, to strengthen his own position, and casting doubt on his brothers. He constantly rubbing his favourite status in his brother's faces. He's not a nice person. This is not a nice approach to doing family.

Let's be honest – their family life to this point has been fairly dysfunctional. Conflict has been the norm. Joseph's brothers, all of them, co-exist with varying degrees of intensity of hate and jealousy towards Joseph and are quite willing to air it. They have nothing nice to say; they pick on him and bully him.

It seems this pulls Joseph closer to his father for relief. Then, to top it off, Dad gifts Joseph with an ornate robe. This is the infamous coat of many colours! It is a robe of status and lavish affection.

A garment for a prince or a noble, not a shepherd, when sheep was the family business. It is a symbol of elitism, a sign of who is in and who is out. It is a message that Joseph is in, and the others are out. And Joseph, as a 17-year-old, laps it up. Joseph' had issues, no doubt about that either. Yet God is present in his story.

Have I thought my own issues disqualify me from experiencing God's presence in my life?

What is it like to consider the presence of God is with me in all situations?

Bible Reading
Genesis 37:5-11

Dreams or Destiny? Joseph revelled in the recital

Joseph has a dream, a significant dream, it obviously made a huge impact on him. It is a God-given dream, we know that, and it was given, not for the 'then', but as encouragement for the future when the troughs were coming.

What things has God given me in the past... that is to hold me in good stead for the present or the future?

The context of the dream is something that is call "primogeniture" [i]
Primogeniture was the legal basis of inheritance that goes to the eldest son. This has been part of European culture for centuries. Primogeniture in Hebrew culture is later defined by Moses to mean that a double portion (as opposed to everything) goes to the eldest son as a resource to support the role of taking on the responsibility and headship of the family. In Deuteronomy 21:17, Moses lays down the requirement that even the first-born son of an unloved wife, must be considered for this role. However, this account is generations prior to this legal clarity. In Jacob's time, primogeniture meant that the estate and responsibility went to the first-born son, and other family members would be gifted with portions of the estate at the father's discretion.
The line of primogeniture becomes messy in this family because it is apparent that Joseph is favoured to usurp the position of 'first born' as the son of Jacob's first son of Rachel – his love and intended wife, not Leah – the older sister, who was deceptively slipped into his marriage bed on his wedding night. Jacob's gift to Joseph of his ornate robe was

> communicating Jacob's decision to have Joseph as his successor as his firstborn. It is little wonder his brother's hated Joseph so much because he threatened their very existence and livelihood.

It appears to Joseph that this prophetic dream is confirming his line of succession as the first-born, and he is not discreet about it. He revels in the recital of all the details. "I had a dream!"

Although we know from other stories of Joseph's life, that he has been given the gift of God to be able to interpret dreams. This is the first encounter that he has with this spiritual gift, and he doesn't seem to handle it graciously. He doesn't just give the account of a harvest, come to life, in full colour Pixar animation but he also knows what this dream means. He knew that he was *that* particular sheaf, and those *other* sheaves were his brothers. He knew that he was standing up in a place of authority, and they were bowing low in an attitude of servitude.

This is a lesson on how to alienate your already estranged siblings even more. Nothing that I read about Joseph in this moment is gracious or tentative or humble. He is arrogant, brash, and conceited. He is quite prepared to step in and take over the family business and become the head of the household.

Have I ever revelled in sharing my good stories, as a way to make other people feel small?

How might I do that in conversation, on social media, or the way I manipulate the data?

How could I share the good things God has given me to encourage others, rather than flaunting it?

Rebuked by his father

Then he has another dream. It is a version of the first dream; different characters, same plot. This time the sun, moon and the stars, are bowing down to Joseph. Not just his brothers, but his father and maternal figures in his life. This was even too much for his father. And Jacob, perhaps for the first time in his life, pulls Joseph into line and rebukes him. Now he is presuming to take this role as head of the household while his father is alive.

All of the messages of Joseph's life that he had been given to this point, did not equip him to handle this matter with diplomacy or skill. He has no filter. The barb of Joseph's attitude drives his brother's hate deeper and deeper, into a vile state of jealousy.

Reminder of destiny

Joseph's dreams are both *symbolic* and *prophetic* in their messages. In the first dream God uses the images of the harvest, which we can see with the privilege of hindsight, that there is a wonderful connection to the season of harvest that Joseph would oversee in Egypt, to save lives right across the known world.

In the second dream God uses the images of the Sun, moon and stars. Egyptians were worshippers of the Sun god Ra, and other celestial bodies. Yet here they are, bowing low to Joseph who is the carrier of the Spirit of Jehovah, the God of his fathers: Abraham, Isaac and Jacob, into a place that did not recognise Jehovah God's sovereignty. How cleverly engineered are the messages of God!

Joseph missed the layers of destiny, his life has only revolved around his father and his business, and this is all he knew. But God gives Joseph these dreams at *this* time, now, for good reason. These dreams were something for him to hold onto as a reminder of God-given, God-imparted destiny. Down the track Joseph needed to know, that God is the God, of *both* the *ridges* and *troughs*, the high points and the low points. Even if it would take him a long time to understand the depths of this truth, God is starting to plant those anchor points in his life now.

Joseph, at this time, is living at home like a prince. He is his father's favourite son. He is in line to inherit everything. He is indulged and pampered. He is living on a ridge. It is a highpoint. It is easy. It is privileged. He even saw his dreams as supporting evidence of his situation of privilege. Life is good.

Yet... if we are honest, Joseph is not showing his best side. For me this is an uncomfortable start to a remarkable life. The high point, the ridge in his life at this time, is not reflective of a good character, or godly engagement with the God of Abraham, Isaac or Jacob. Our responsibility is not just to ride the ridges and to avoid the troughs, but to do life with God, whether it is high or whether it is low. Whether it is hard or whether it flows smoothly.

Some Final thoughts...

We live in a world that offers life with ridges and troughs. Without exception, we experience high points and low points. But our lives as followers of Jesus is not about being able to stay on top of the ridges, but to experience God, in all of these times. God is not measuring the success of our lives by height of our ridges or the depth of our troughs but our awareness of God in all and any of these times.

The job that God spoke to me about, was in a warehouse. It was with Christian Worship Music organisation. I was offered the role of being their national production manager, and their major accounts manager. It was a big step up from the administrative experience that I had at that time. There was so much to learn. Budgets to manage. Customers to engage. Production timelines to keep on track. Product stock levels to monitor.

*One day, I was in the photocopier room, and I became completely overwhelmed. I understand now that I was basically having a panic attack. I couldn't do this! God, what was I thinking? As I'm standing at the photocopier; trying not to pass out; trying not to run for my car-keys and never some back, God brought the voice of a gentle lady back to my mind. "God wants you to know that you are the right person for the job, for this season, that you **can** do it because God has positioned you there.'*

Ahh... I could breathe...

When I received that message, it felt like a ridge moment. Yaah! Exhilarating and affirming. When I needed that message, it was definitely a trough moment. I was hanging on for dear life, trying not to drown. Yet God was present in both those moments: not one more so, than the other. He was present, helping me to keep going.

Can you think of a time when you or someone you know, was reminded that God is with us whether we are experiencing a ridge or a trough?

We will see how Joseph experienced God, doing life together, on the ridges and in the troughs.

Prayer:

Father God, it is a good reminder to know that you are with us whether things are going well, or whether we are struggling. Thank you that you are with us. That you help us, give us strength and wisdom and resource. Help us to walk through all of our times with grace and integrity. Forgive us for the times we have accused you of abandoning us when we hit a trough. Thank you that you do not exclude us on the basis of how well life is going, but you love us consistently. If you are with us, we are blessed indeed.
In Jesus' name, Amen.

2.

The Trough of Slavery

Where we have been...

As we have been reflecting on the idea of ridges and troughs like the natural profile that we see in the sand at the beach. The ups and the downs of the landscape of our lives. Sometimes life is positive and progressing and moving, doors opening, opportunities coming at us. But sometimes things are hard, like ploughing through mud, being sucked down, trying to make headway and not quite making it.

As we consider the life of Joseph through this lens, we see that Joseph's life was full of ridges and troughs. Extremely high places and very deep low places. Yet his success as a person was not defined by the height of the ridges, but it was his connectedness to God, how he continued faithfully with God, regardless of the ridges and regardless of the troughs. That was his success.

What is the nature of some of my troughs?

Now we look at the very deep trough that Joseph is thrown into.

Bible Reading
Genesis 37:12-30

Hate escalated

The brothers are away shepherding. Droving to support their animals and their livelihood, to find pasture for their sheep.

Jacob sends Joseph to his brothers. This is a big journey and a significant responsibility of trust to carry out alone as a young person. The trip on foot to Shecham is 78 km; Dothan is 22 km further north of Shecham. Joseph is stepping out into the big boys' territory. He is moving from being the boy at home, into the responsibility of a man, possibly even responsibility as the first born, over the others.

No wonder he was keen, and willing to go. But remember that Joseph is hated by his brothers. Joseph has given Jacob reports before, and he has not been in the habit of reporting positively that all is well with his brothers. He hasn't given impartial accounts, or positive ones.

Yet here, Jacob explicitly enlists Joseph to report on his brothers. The intent is to go and get a report. "Go and see", "bring back a report". When his brothers spot Joseph's bright and colourful coat walking across the paddock towards them, there is a very strong reaction!
"Here comes that dreamer!"
"Let's kill him!"
"We'll see what will come of his grandiose designs then!"
They see a way to restore the status quo and reestablish security in their future. The finger of hate has escalated to a point that they choose to pull the trigger of revenge, and it is rooted in their disgust. Years and years of escalating jealousy and distrust erupts into this violent plan of revenge.

Joseph quite literally falls into a trough. In one moment, he goes from being the favoured son and heir: from being on a special assignment –

living on a ridge, to being held and incarcerated in an empty well. Jospeh falls straight into a very deep trough.

Reuben advocates

Reuben steps in. He is the actual first born of Jacob. The oldest son to Leah. All his life, he has been trained and anticipating his succession to the household. Even in this situation he advocates for Joseph's life. He wants to return Joseph home and reconcile him to his father.

And my questions is: why is Reuben so determined to advocate for Joseph? Is he just a nicer person? Did he have less of a problem with Joseph, and his favouritism, and his big noting? Did he not want the job as first-born?

Perhaps Reuben's training as the first born instilled in him not just the position of privilege but also the 'obligation'[ii] this role held. It was the firstborn who was given the priestly responsibility of the family. The birthright was a baton of *authority* and *responsibility* of the household that was placed into the hands of the firstborn. The firstborn was the person, who would hold headship over the family when the father passed on. He was also the one you would come to if there were debts to be settled, or disputes to be sorted, or justice to be obtained.

The role of firstborn carried this obligation and responsibility to administer justice, not just the privilege for having the good luck than having the birth order of being the oldest. This picture of the firstborn, in our spiritual lives in also found in Jesus. Jesus is the firstborn in our spiritual family: he has carried our justice; he has become our advocate.

Paul explains it this way:
Bible Reading
Colossians 1:15-22

Jesus carried the justice required of the firstborn. We are reconciled to our father God through him. In Jacob's family, Reuben, who to this point had been raised as the firstborn, and he is advocating for Joseph's life, as the carrier of justice. If this crime ever came to light, as the next 'firstborn' he would be required to carry the justice of this situation. It could possibly mean he would carry the sentence of death for death.

Even before the Mosaic law was instituted, tribal justice was as rudimentary as an eye for an eye, and a life for a life. Reuben's solution is to placate his brothers, stick Joseph down a hole to retrieve him later and return him to his father.

Good plan.

Brothers retaliated

But the plan goes belly-up when Reuben does not share their meal when they stop for lunch. There is a tradition[iii] that suggests Reuben was fasting and repenting because of this sin, which is in line with the priestly role of the firstborn, and that is why he was not eating with the others. Regardless as to why, we know that Reuben is not there, and Judah sees a caravan of merchants are passing by on their way to Egypt with a cargo of spices from the Gilead foothills.
Judah sees the solution to a couple of problems:
- Joseph would be eliminated.
- The line of succession would be reinstated to what it had been.
- They would extract their revenge.
- They wouldn't have blood on their hands like they would if they murdered him.
- They would keep their consciences clean from harming their brother.
- And, they would make some money on the side.

So, the brothers sell their brother for twenty shekels of silver.

Are there situations where I am looking for retribution, or revenge?

Twenty shekels of silver...
Many people have drawn parallels of Joseph's betrayal to the betrayal of Jesus who was betrayed and sold for 30 pieces of silver, by one of his band of brothers.

Thirty shekels was the base price of a slave in the Mosaic law. Because Joseph was a minor at seventeen years of age, he was sold for the lower price of twenty shekels. A shepherd in this era might earn eight shekels a year, so this is equivalent to two and a half years wages [iv].

Joseph is at the bottom of a deep trough and sold as a slave. Strangers – traders passing by, join in this plot and take advantage of him for profit. He begs for his life, and his pleas go unheeded. Later on, the brothers remember the anguish that Joseph experienced as they betrayed their brother when he was tied up and sold like goods at a market.

Have I experience betrayal that has turned my life upside down?

Bible Reference
Genesis 42:21

Now Joseph is no longer a prince. Now, he is not even considered a person. Now, he is someone's property, a belonging, somebody's stuff. Now, worthless, not valued, and no good. Joseph has gone from living on a ridge as the favoured son of his father and fallen into the trough of slavery. It is deep. It is wide. Potentially it is life-long. There is nothing to suggest at this point, Joseph will be anything else, other than someone else's property for the rest of his life.

Bible Reading
Genesis 37:5-11

Collaborate

Reuben discovers this turn of events, when he returns to find Joseph gone, and he is absolutely distraught. If we allow the idea that Reuben is still mindful of his first-born obligations, it makes sense why Reuben is so distressed. Reuben is looking down the barrel of being called to account for his brother's death, on behalf of his brothers. "Where can I turn now?" he demands in despair. In reality, Reuben had nowhere to turn. Justice means he would be held to account. Eye for an eye; life for a life. So, his brother's step in and collaborate with a plan.

Coverup

They create a coverup. They produce evidence of a different tragedy. They slaughtered a goat and used its blood to create sufficient conjecture that Joseph had been attacked by a wild animal. They use his distinctive custom-made coat as an item they found, tattered and bloodstained.

Their deception is skilled and effective. They allow Jacob to draw the obvious conclusions himself. And then Jacob, who during his early life was known as the deceiver, is now deceived.

Bible Reference
Genesis 25:19-34; 27:1-41

Consequences

The thing about buying in to revenge and payback, is that the consequences are long lasting and wide. Joseph is gone, but the brothers live with the echoes of their betrayal.

Jacob falls into deep, complicated, intractable grief. His own trough of despair engulfs him. Nothing lifts him out of it. It is not like Jacob now chooses another favourite son; instead, he retracts, and they witness their father waste away in his grief.

Jacob even makes a very sad vow: that he will never be comforted and rather than heal, he will remain in this state of intense mourning until he dies himself.

Although we can definitely acknowledge Joseph contributed to the estrangement of his brothers, this story is not about laying blame.

> *We had a very strong sense that God was moving us to a new community. That sounds exciting, but then there's the logistics of making that happen: shifting from schools, jobs, creating new networks, and even establishing ourselves with a different faith community.*
>
> *The challenges are often different in different situations, and the hardest thing this time was finding a house to live in which was affordable. Every time we disclosed we had four children under the age of 10, suddenly houses were not available. I was pretty confident that if I had had four dogs, instead of children, our applications would have been considered more benevolently.*
>
> *I remember being so distressed and crying to God, "What am I doing wrong here?" I was praying and praying and there seemed a lot of silence. This was a trough for me. I remember talking to people about*

our struggle. But I notice looking back, I assumed the trough needed to be attributed some blame somewhere, and I had a default position where I took that onto myself.

Nor is Joseph's story about determining "why" trough experiences happen. It is more compelling to explore the "how" questions:
- *How* did Joseph manage it to get through this trough?
- *How* did he keep going and not give up?
- *How* was he able to stay close to God in spite of the bottom falling out of his life?
- *How* was God using this trough for something that was good?

What is my usual way of dealing with a trough?

Am I someone who turns their face to the wall, and gives up?

Am I more inclined to ask "why?" or "how?"

These are the questions we will look for as we continue to look at Joseph's experiences. What we do know is that this trough was used by God to position Joseph for good. God wanted to position Joseph in Egypt, another nation, another culture. This trough was the portal in which God used to move Joseph to Egypt.

Some final thoughts...

Joseph lived and experienced high points and low points. Here, he has gone from a ridge point to a very deep trough, very suddenly.

As I have thought about our inability to find a suitable home in the story I shared earlier, in hindsight I can see that we were not doing anything wrong. Yes, I was frustrated but we had the support of a great friend. Yes, it was hard, living out of a single room with four young children, but now I can see God was positioning our family for a significant time in our life. When we found a house, we were only in that neighbourhood for a short period, about 18 months, but I can see God positioned us there. Intentionally. The trough I experienced was not about doing something wrong, even though, in my thinking, I had a default position to believe that a trough was probably because I was not praying enough, or Christian enough. I no longer think like that. The trough was, in fact, about timing and positioning.

So, at another time in our life, when we had to move and things were not meshing together, I was able to remind myself: sometimes the trough is a trough, required to perfect the timing, or to perfect the positioning. I was able to use this story to remind myself. Yes, I have checked my conscience to check if there are personal things I need to attend to, and then I was able to trust God in the trough.

How could I be more balanced in assessing what is happening during a trough experience?

This trough which Joseph fell into was a much more difficult and extreme experience. It was unexpected. It was betrayal. It was intense. It was unjust.

And sometimes troughs are like that, they are unexpected betrayals that are intense and unjust. In the story of Joseph, we have the privilege of seeing some of "how". "How" he managed to live in and through this trough, as traumatic, and as difficult, and as deep, as it was. We get to see how Joseph doesn't turn his face to the wall and give up. He continues on and somehow, this trough is used by God as part of his sovereign plan to position him for God's purposes, in unlikely places, in Egypt. Slavery did not have the last word. Betrayal did not have the last word. Hate and jealousy did not have the last word. Strangers and profit-making did not have the last word.

God is always present in both the ridge moments and the trough moments, not one, more so, than the other.

What is it like to remind myself, God is with me... even in deep troughs?

God is present in both, helping us, positioning us, empowering us to keep going. That is what is important: doing life *with* God on the ridges and in the troughs.

Prayer:

Father God, thank you that your presence is a constant in our lives, regardless of whether in the moment it is a ridge or a trough. Thank you that we can trust You in those places that You have not abandoned us; that your purposes will be achieved and in actual fact sometimes you choose to use trough moments as a way of delivering your purposes. That is hard for us to get our head around, when we are in the thick of a trough experience. Help us to turn our eyes and ears towards you in these times.
In Jesus' name, Amen.

3.
The Ridge of Stewardship

Where we have been...

Joseph has gone from the favoured ridge of being his father's firstborn son of privilege, to plunging into a very deep low trough when his brothers betray him and sell him as a slave.

Now Joseph engages with his reality of being a slave. He engages with life in that trough, until it forms into a ridge.

Bible Reading
Genesis 39:1-5

Presence of the Lord

Slavery does not seem like a place that can be turned into a ridge but this is what we see happens. A series of events happen to position Joseph in a place of influence.

He is bought by an Egyptian. This is not just any Egyptian, but one who is an official, the captain of the guard, a man of military position. Potiphar is one of Pharoah's trusted men. He oversees the military might of the Egyptian army.

Egypt is the political world power of this era; not just by trade, negotiation and political strategy, but by having the meanest army around. Potiphar was a man with social and political clout. Yet what we notice is that it is not the *position* of Potiphar that is the nature of this turn around in Joseph's life, but Joseph's awareness of the Presence of the Lord.

Do I feel that I need someone to blame, or to at least take responsibility before I can move on or climb out of my trough?

The presence of the Lord went with Joseph, through the trough into the ridge where we see Joseph positioned with greater influence.

One of the ideas that I came across when I became ordained as a pastor and received my pastoral credential, was that somehow, I had "arrived". Another pastor said to me, "I am so excited that now we are now doing ministry together!"
That comment disturbed me because we had been working together for over ten years. I think I was so definite about the way I viewed this because the Holy Spirit had already spoken to me that my credential was "Not about the position but about positioning." This credential was something that supported my positioning where God needed me.

God is intentional in the positioning of all of his people. Sometimes that will look positive and affirming, sometimes it will even include the appointment to a position. The invitation in the story of Joseph for us, is to consider that sometimes that positioning might look quite different.

Positioned for Success

Joseph is still a slave. He is still considered property. But even within that limitation, now he has an opportunity to shine. Task by task, job by job, Joseph demonstrates his God-given, God-anointed capacity. Each time he completes an assignment well, he builds credibility, and it creates momentum.

Joseph impresses Potiphar to the point where he appoints him as his personal attendant. Joseph is a man who had to learn a new language: both spoken and written. He had to adapt to a new culture, a new way of doing life, not as a free man, but as a slave. This role is a ridge in comparison to being chained in a slave-gang in a Ishmaelites camel train.

Rather than stay in a place of bitterness and resentment over the betrayal he experienced at the hand of his brothers, Joseph gets on with life. Joseph manages with integrity what God gives him access to. He works to demonstrate his capacity and ability. And as he does, Potiphar offers more and more opportunity to Joseph.

>More and more success is demonstrated.
>More and more achievements are realised.
>More and more goals are kicked.

And soon we see Joseph is not just a personal butler, but now he is the head steward, over the entire household and then over Potiphar's entire estate.

When I experience a ridge of influence, am I inclined to think I deserve it, or that I am entitled to it because I have worked by own way up the ladder?

A man of Potiphar's position would have had significant holdings Joseph managed all his internal and external matters. In the house, and in the field. He demonstrates his organisational skills, his administrative skill, his people skills, his financial management, his business management capacity.

When the Bible says, *"The Lord was with Joseph"*, does this mean that God wasn't with him before in the trough – when his brothers betrayed him? No! God was with him then as well, but this success was God given and God appointed. God positioned for success. This wasn't a matter of Joseph clawing his way out. This was a case of God's positioning as much as any other.

Potiphar is blessed... because of Joseph

With all of Joseph's attention to detail, came unprecedented prosperity and success to Potiphar's household *because* the Lord was with him. What we see, is that Joseph carries the presence of God with him into an ungodly place and that place is transformed.

Everything that Potiphar has, is now blessed, from the time that Joseph was in the house. Joseph is described as being the conduit of blessing, because he carries with him the presence of the Lord.

We are told that the Lord blessed the Potiphar's household because of Joseph. Because of... This is cause and effect. Joseph had an awareness of the presence of God. The Lord was with him. He carried the presence of God with him as he went about his duties in Potiphar's house. And because of that, Potiphar experienced a season of unprecedented blessing. Inside and outside, Joseph has unusual success, as he stewards his master's household.

It seems even Potiphar acknowledges that this is a divine and unusual blessing that has come his way. The conjecture would be that this was different *before* Joseph arrived, and it was different *after* Joseph leaves. Perhaps this unusual blessing of prosperity leaves with him. How else would they be able to draw the connection with Joseph and the prosperity God freely blessed this household with during this season.

Bible Reading
Genesis 39:6-10

Integrity

What becomes very obvious in this story is the integrity in which Joseph fulfils his roles. He didn't cut corners. In all matters he demonstrated his oversight with reliability. So much so that Potiphar no longer checks up on him. There was no need. He lets Joseph take care of everything. Joseph executes his duties with diligence and integrity. All Potiphar needs to worry about when and what he will eat.

Oh, happy day when Potiphar bought Joseph from the slave market.

Then we see Joseph's integrity is tested. When he addresses Potiphar's wife, he not only declares it would be a betrayal of the trust that his master has generously given him, but that it would also be a betrayal against God.

Here we see written for the first time, in black and white, the priority that Joseph gives to God – the God of Abraham, Isaac and his father Jacob. This is the motivating source of strength in his life.

How strong is my integrity quota?

Am I tempted to fudge the rules or moral lines?

Intentions

What I notice that in spite of what is thrown at Joseph, he stays on track. He is not seduced by the position, or the prosperity, or the success. He is not seduced by idea that he could be more, but demonstrates over and over his faithfulness to the role that he now has. He stays aware that Potiphar is the 'Master', and that he is the 'slave'.

There is no thought that he could use Potiphar's wife as revenge or pay back. There is no entertaining the flattery that his wife thought he was handsome and well built. There is no thought that he could become more than his station by going behind his master's back and into his master's bedroom.

There is a little aside in Chapter 35, before the account of Joseph's betrayal, that concerns Joseph's oldest brother, Reuben.

Bible Reference
Genesis 35:22

Reuben was Israel's firstborn. We considered the responsibility that comes with primogeniture, the role and position of firstborn. Yet here Reuben took what was not his, his father's wife and slept with her. Was this Reuben's design to be more? Was this his attempt to demonstrate his position and authority in the household?

The result of this betrayal was that Reuben lost his birthright and his life became barren, not in a physical sense, he had a family but there was a restraint over his life. On his deathbed Jacob declares that where Reuben had previously excelled, he would no longer excel, and the birthright is passed to Judah.

Bible Reference
Genesis 49:1-12

What we do notice is that there were no significant judges, or kings from the tribe of Reuben. Nothing exceptional, nothing that excels. This was also the sin of Absalom – the son of King David. As a ploy to abdicate his father from the throne, his advisors intentionally pitched a tent on the palace roof to advertise what they were doing, Absalom was taking over the role of authority, by taking his father's wives.

Bible Reference
2 Samuel 16:21–22

Absalom had intentions that were outside his designation. Joseph, however, did not go there. He stayed away from sliding into that mindset. He was not seduced by the idea that he was worth more or entitled to more. He stays aware that Potiphar is the person of authority, and he has a delegated role. He doesn't become seduced by the idea of grandiose designs of arrogance.

There are no longer any echoes of that 17-year-old youth who was boasting about his dreams. Here we have a man, humbled by the troughs of his life, and holding himself with great dignity even while walking high on the ridge of stewardship

Insistent

Potiphar's wife, however, is indulged and insistent. She will not be put off. She has set her eyes on Joseph and will not take 'no' for an answer. She has no loyalty or faithfulness to her husband, and no sense that this is a bad idea that will not end well.

So, she harasses Joseph and sensibly he stays out of her way and refuses to even be with her.

What is my way of dealing with harassment?

Bible Reading
Genesis 39: 11-20

Enticed

Over and over Potiphar's wife tried to entice Joseph into crossing his own moral compass. Over and over and over. And yet he holds his ground and does not give way.

Then she lies in wait, as it were, waiting for a time, a place and an opportunity. A time when she could take what she coveted. What I notice is Joseph's quiet strength, no sexual harassment claims, just quiet avoidance and getting on with his job.

Entrapped

Then she finds her moment, no witnesses, no barriers. This is the perfect opportunity to get away with doing the wrong thing. But it is also the perfect opportunity for her to flip on a dime. Joseph's rejection turns Potiphar's wife's desire into disgust. She frames him for the crime he has persistently avoided.

Joseph has no alibi. No witness. No legal standing. No rights.

Did you notice the irony that it is Joseph's cloak that once again gets him into trouble? This cloak of stewardship was associated with a ridge season, just has his father's colourful coat was.

Have I experienced betrayal that has turned my life upside down?

Potiphar's wife holds his cloak as evidence that he had attempted to rape her. It is again used to collaborate a situation using deceit and injustice.

Enraged

Potiphar is enraged by her story. He takes Joseph and incarcerates him in the Egyptian prison. He throws Joseph into the dungeon where Pharoah's prisoners were kept. Joseph doesn't get a right of reply, or legal representation. This is unjust, unfair, unwarranted. Again.

Yet, the rage of Potiphar is not the sovereign force at play here. Again, we see whether on the ridge or in the trough, God's sovereignty is more powerful. It is more powerful than a woman's manipulation and her plots to frame. It is more powerful than a man's fury, and his hunger for revenge.

Where have I been bombarded by someone's fury and rage when I was not at fault?

Some say it is remarkable that Joseph wasn't executed for these charges. A military man like Potiphar, would have found this situation humiliating. Perhaps the design of Potiphar, was that he would go right to the top to have Joseph publicly executed.

Joseph has gone from the ridge of being a respected steward, to now being a convicted criminal in an Egyptian prison. The person that he faithfully served, and worked hard for, the person he was a conduit of blessing for, now throws him in prison.

This is a deep trough Joseph finds himself in again. And yet even here God's sovereignty prevails.

Deserving Ridges?

Joseph has gone from the very deep trough of slavery to a ridge of respectable stewardship. Joseph builds his credibility through his integrity and demonstrates his capacity. And eventually he is appointed as the head steward of a very influential official in Egypt.

Let's be honest: we like the ridge experiences. Joseph is blessed. In this position, he was a conduit of blessing as he works in this man's estate.
>It was unexpected.
>It was prosperous.
>It was successful.
>It was a platform to develop and expand Joseph's ability and capacity and he does it with integrity.

That feels right, it feels appropriate, that through God's positioning, a slave can rise to such a station of influence. And sometimes ridges are like that, they happen. They are unexpected appointments, full of blessing.

Yet somehow, we want to deserve the blessing and avoid the troughs. But Joseph doesn't forget that in this place, it is a place where he has been positioned by God. The blessing is in the *presence* of God and that is available to us in the high, and even in the low places. Joseph continues on with integrity and allows this ridge was to be used by God as part of God's sovereign plan to position Joseph for His purposes in unlikely places, even in the home of an influential Egyptian official.

What Joseph is learning is that his success as a person, was not so much about the height of the ridges or the accomplishment of his position, but how he continued faithfully with God, regardless of the ridges and regardless of the troughs.

How do I define success and failure?

I found a diagram that articulated this very clearly for me, and it was compiled by Dr John Warlow, a Christian psychiatrist.[v]

Defining Success and Failure

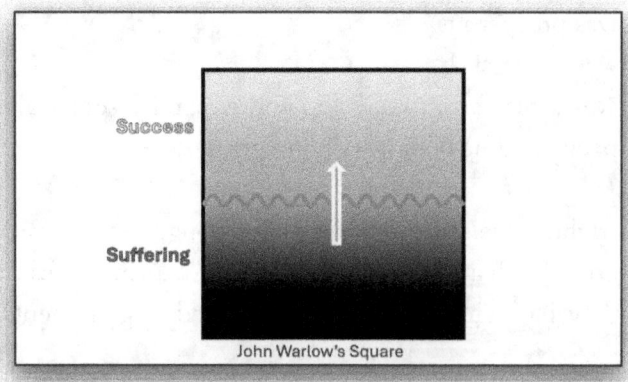

Success is often defined as staying above the waterline the place that rises above suffering. It might be physical success in our health, or financial success as opposed to debt, or social success and influential success. It considers that when we are on the ridge, we are successful. Likewise, we often identify that suffering, equates to being below the water line, finding ourselves in a trough that suffering in all sorts of areas in our lives equates with failure.

The Lens of Self-centred or God-centred lives

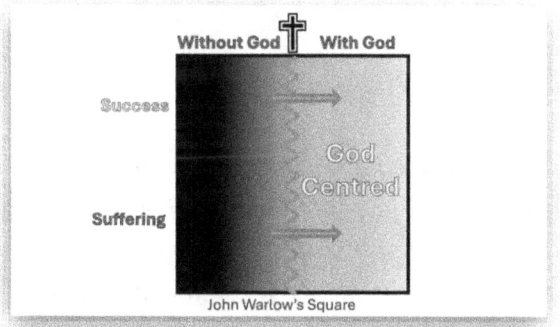

God centred Lives are successful lives

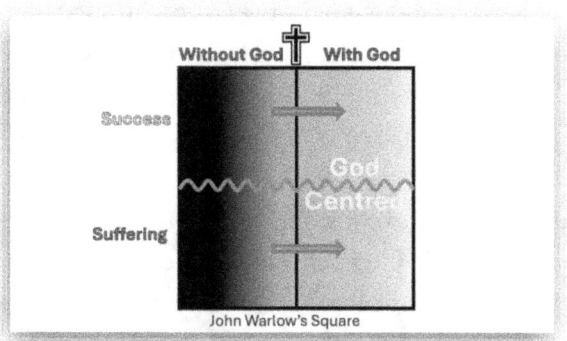

God invites us to look at life through a different lens, through a lens that considers whether we are doing life "with" God or "without" him.

Success in God's eyes is not the height of the ridge or the depth of the trough, but our awareness that God is in the centre of our experience... regardless of where we are in relation to the waterline.

Is this way of looking at success and failure comfortable or uncomfortable for me?

Some final thoughts

Remarkably Joseph was able to define his success in different ways to what we might usually find. Even on the ridge of stewardship to stay God-centred. He wasn't seduced by this position he hadn't considered that he had arrived and somehow now he was entitled to more. He did well, with what was placed in his hand because God remained at the centre of this ridge experience.

Potiphar and his political clout did not have the last word. Potiphar's wife and her betrayal did not have the last word. God is always present in both the ridge moments and the trough moments, not one, more than the other. Our job is to build our awareness of God in both places, helping us, positioning us, empowering us to keep going.

The invitation in the life of Joseph is to follow his example and to strive to life in a way that is God-centred, God conscious, God honouring, doing life *with* God, regardless of whether we are above or below the water line, on the ridge or in the trough. This is the definition of a life well lived; this is God's definition of success.

This is what is important: Doing life with God, regardless of the ridges or the troughs.

Prayer:

Father God, thank you for the reminder that regardless of what this week looks like, that your presence is with us. Thank you, Holy Spirit, that you are loving us and teaching us to be more mindful of who you are and helping us, where you have positioned us. Help us to be like Joseph, to be conduits of blessing in the places where we work, for your glory and honour.
In Jesus Name, Amen.

4.

The Trough of Suffering

Where we have been...

Joseph has stepped out of the trough of being sold as a slave to being highly regarded with a position of influence and responsibility as the head steward of Potiphar's estate. He flourishes on this ridge, until he is falsely accused by his jealous wife. Now his reality is that he is not just a slave but a slave who is also a convicted felon, incarcerated in an Egyptian dungeon.

I remember writing to a friend in prison. Yes, he was charged and convicted of a felony. I remember being profoundly impacted by the idea, that like Joseph, for this season he was in prison. And I wondered how would I manage this if, through circumstances that were direct consequences of my choices, or even outside my control, how would I manage if I was positioned in prison?
Can God take something so deep, suffering so overwhelming, and use that for his purposes?

Bible Reading
Genesis 39:20-23

Experienced Kindness

Prison does not seem a likely place of blessing, but this is what we see happens. We have been considering the idea that rather than defining blessing as ridge experiences when things are going well, that blessing is, in fact, from the presence of the Lord, the Lord is with us. God-centred rather than self-centred, regardless of whether we are experiencing life as a ridge or a trough.

Joseph is condemned to an Egyptian prison. But not just any Egyptian prison, but this prison was Pharaoh's official prison, where those who have offended the king were incarcerated. So, regardless of the fact that Joseph has never directly served Pharoah, he was interred with those who have served and spoken to the king, such was Potiphar's influence and high rank to put him there.

But just because this is the king's prison, I do not take this to mean it was a place of comfort. This was still an Egyptian prison in the 1700's BC – this is not a nice place. It is a prison; Joseph describes it as a "dungeon". This is a place where Joseph was thrown and discarded, without cause.

The injustice of a situation adds depth to our troughs of suffering. We can perceive things differently if there is a sense that we deserve what is happening. Joseph did not deserve this. He had done his job well. He had worked with integrity. Yet here he is plummeting into this trough of injustice, condemnation, suffering, oppression and abuse.

Yet scripture tells us that even here Joseph is blessed *because* the Lord was with him. *The Lord was with him.* The presence of the Lord transforms a place of suffering into a place where Joseph experiences kindness.

When I experience a trough of suffering, how am I able to focus on God's presence as blessing in that place?

God granted him *kindness*.

If we look at how other translations have expressed this Hebrew word for kindness: *kheh'-sed*, we find words such as:
> Kindness
> Gracious love
> Mercy
> Steadfast love
> Was good to him
> Lovingkindness

Regardless of the place, regardless of the trough of suffering God's presence extends kindness, gracious love, mercy, steadfast love, was good to him, shows lovingkindness to Joseph.

Joseph is now not just a slave, he is a condemned prisoner. But even within this extreme limitation, he encounters the kindness of God.

Encountered favour

Even in this situation, this kindness of God means Joseph is granted the favour of the prison warden. Job by job, task by task, Joseph demonstrates his God-given, God-anointed capacity.

I have speculated about the types of jobs that would be given to a prisoner, in a 1700 BC prison. I have not found any resources to help me here, but I am going to suggest that they were messy, unsavoury, unglamorous tasks. It may have included dealing with the toilet waste, or dressing the wounds of prisoners, or the distribution of rations, or acting as an umpire if there were disgruntled disputes.

Whatever was required, Joseph gets in and does *that*. Each time he does something well, it builds credibility, it creates momentum, it creates trust. Joseph impresses the prison warden to the point where he puts him in charge. This role is a rough trough when compared to being the head steward of Potiphar's estate.

Rather than stay in a place of bitterness and resentment over the betrayal he experienced at the hand of Potiphar's wife, Joseph gets on with life where he currently is.

Extended responsibility

Joseph manages with integrity what God has given him access to. He works to demonstrate his capacity and ability. As he does, the warden offers more and more responsibility to Joseph. Soon we see Joseph is not just a prisoner, but now he has been given responsibility over the other prisoners, and then over the entire prison and all that was done there. This warden held a position of significant responsibility – he answered to Pharoah for his prisoners.

It seems to me that God is flexing and training Joseph's organisational skills; his administrative skill; his people skills; his financial management; his business management capacity. And now Joseph is addressing administrative matters and developing his managerial capacity in a very different context to Potiphar's tidy estate.

With Joseph's attention to detail, the warden extended responsibility to him *because* the Lord was with him. Joseph is described as having success in whatever he did, *because of* the presence of the Lord. *Because of*, again, this is cause and effect. This is not just Joseph clawing his way to the top because he was a compulsive Type A personality. This is God's grace, with him in the trough, releasing him to be everything God had created him to be, even in the circumstance of a prison, even in the context of suffering.

That happens because Joseph carries the presence of God with him. He carried integrity into an ungodly place and that place is transformed. He carried light into a dark place and that place is transformed. He carried salt into an unsavoury place and that place is transformed. He carried care into a hurting place and that place is transformed. Everything that this prison was, is experiencing blessing and transformation, from the time that Joseph was incarcerated.

Bible Reading
Genesis 40:1-8

Trough of Waiting

Joseph is in a trough of suffering and waiting. The suffering here, may not be physical pain, as he steps into an overseer role, but the fact remains, he is incarcerated. He is locked up. I believe Joseph is convinced God will get him out of the trough of this prison, but at the moment he is in a holding pattern of waiting.

We read that '*sometime later, after he had been in custody for some time...*'. This was not all done and dusted in a fortnight; this was an extended period, most likely years. Joseph was seventeen when he arrived in Egypt as a slave; he was thirty when he got out of prison and appointed into the king's service. Although we don't know how long he was in Potiphar's service, his time in prison was an extended period of suffering.

Taking a step back

I've mentioned that we can get caught up in the 'why?" questions when things are difficult. It is more compelling and more helpful to consider the 'how' questions. *How* did Joseph manage his trough experience? *How* did he keep going? I think in this passage we are offered some insight into the *how*. Not just *how* Joseph survived this trough but *how* did he thrive there?

Perhaps one aspect of this was his ability to take a step back, and to consider the perspective from God's sovereignty. Perhaps he was able to frame this trough season as a 'training' for what was next. God had already given him a vision and a dream. He understood what those dreams meant since God has given Joseph the spiritual gift of interpreting dreams. Yet to get from *this* point, to *that* point, takes a process. This is not an instant microwaved life that we live.

This involves taking a step back, being able to pause and acknowledge that God has a different perspective to what we might see when we are at the bottom of a trough. If Joseph knew and understood that the interpretations of dreams belonged to God, then the outworking and delivery of those dreams also belongs to God.

Taking care

Joseph didn't cut corners. He took care. In all matters he demonstrated his oversight with reliability and follow-through. He made an effort to see the people behind the criminal charge and the accusation. These people were not numbers on a sheet of allegations.

We are told that Joseph *"attended"* the butler and the baker. He is serving and attending to the people with care, rather than numbers in a cellblock. He may have needed to dress their wounds if they have been flogged. He may have needed to help them orientate to their new environment. This was his style, he cared.

Took time to notice

Did you notice that Joseph *noticed?* Really noticed. He noticed that these two prisoners were out of sorts this morning. He is not dominated by his position of authority, or his lists of things that needed to be done. He notices and takes time to follow-up on what he notices.

It takes time to check in and say, "Hey, what's going on guys, you look upset." It takes time to pause, and to listen, and not be dismissive. It takes time.

How diligent am I in making time for people?

The reality is that Joseph is not going anywhere, he has all the time in the world, but it could have been tempting to feel important and to get caught up with dealing with the other responsibilities and other jobs that he was given charge over.

Joseph however did not dismiss and move on. He takes time. He was here to serve the prisoners. He was not seduced by the idea that he was above the other prisoners, or that his time was worth more than their nightmares. He stays aware that they have common ground, that he is also a prisoner, and they were in this together. Here we have a man, humbled by the troughs of his life, and Joseph holds himself with great dignity even while walking through this low trough of suffering and waiting.

What other pressures demand my attention?

Taking it to God

Both these men had dreams. They have no doubt they are spiritual events, not just their mind processing the trauma of being in an Egyptian prison. Joseph identifies God in this experience and draws their attention to the God factor.

Both men knew their dreams had interpretations, but now they are in prison, and they do not have access to their traditional cultural ways of dealing with this. They could not go and buy the services of the wise magi who would normally attend to these things for them. So, they feel stuck on both accounts: their physical imprisonment, but also the limitations that their spiritual needs could not be met in this place, because they could not go to a temple or a priest that is on the outside.

I love that Joseph gently acknowledges that his *God is not locked out* because they were *locked in.* God is here, in the prison, in the trough. Here. Now. The interpretations belong to God, not wise magicians in heathen temples.

Even here, Joseph deals with what is distressing by taking it to God. We cannot offer to others, what we do not understand or experience ourselves. Joseph was able to offer his support to the cupbearer and the baker because he understood and experienced what it was like to take stuff to God all the time. This happens so naturally and spontaneously. This is familiar ground.

How quick am I to take things to God, or am determined to try something else first?

Bible Reading
Genesis 40: 9-23

The Detail of the Dreams

The details of these dreams are incredible. They are clear. They are disturbing. They are specific. The baker is encouraged by the interpretation Joseph gives the cupbearer, offers the details of his dream also. The detail is equally clear, but this time the meaning is not at all what he wanted to hear.

Definite

We are told the definite outcomes of these men's fates. Be reassured that the dreams did not make what happened to these men occur. Prophetic dreams only provide insight into what *will* happen. It is the symbolic documentation of those events, unveiled beforehand.

This is a specific, accurate account of what these dreams meant for those men. And Joseph is true to the interpretations. He did not hold back delivering the truth of what he understood, just because the second account was gruesome and harsh.

Joseph so believes in the accuracy of what God has revealed, so that he begs the cupbearer to advocate for his position before Pharoah when he is released. But the cupbearer forgot about Joseph. Once he was reinstated and went back to his own position of influence and success, Joseph's kindness, and support, and predicament is lost.

It is very easy to wonder, 'What is the point?' Joseph is still in the dungeon; this trough of suffering is still his experience.

Demonstration

I am convinced that one of the reasons the precise detail of these dreams is recorded for us, is because it provides a powerful and stark demonstration of the power of God to unlock mysteries, even in supernatural ways.

These dreams were a powerful demonstration of God's sovereignty, and his wisdom, and his overarching authority. Although it is not immediately evident, we can step back and see whether we are standing on the ridge or in the bottom of a trough, God's authority is more enduring. More enduring than a gaoler's favour. More enduring than a cupbearer's self-absorbed forgetfulness and his lack of follow through.

Some final thoughts...

Joseph has gone from the ridge of being a respected steward, to now being a convicted criminal in an Egyptian prison. Yet Joseph gets on with using what God has placed in his circle of influence, and builds his capacity by consistently, and with integrity, fulfilling responsibility as opportunity is offered to him.

Eventually he is appointed as the caretaker of this Egyptian prison, to become a conduit of blessing to those entrusted to his care. He is given responsibility and works hard to steward what has been placed in his hand with integrity.

And yet those he tended, and those he worked for, and those cared for, and those he made time for, like the cupbearer who forgot him when he is released from prison and restored to his previous life. He did not bother to advocate for Joseph. This is a deep trough Joseph finds himself in. And yet, even here, God's sovereignty prevails.

Let's be honest: we don't like the trough experiences. This was unfair. This was painful. This was full of suffering. It doesn't feel right or appropriate that someone in a demonstrated position of trust, can be punished for something they did not do. Sometimes troughs are like that: they happen. They are unexpected appointments, full of suffering.

Of course, we want to deserve the blessing and avoid the troughs. But Joseph doesn't forget God's perspective, that even in this place, this is a place where God is with him.

The blessing is in the *presence* of God and that is available to us, even in the low places. But again, even this trough became a platform to develop and expand Joseph's ability and capacity. Joseph continues on and allows this trough to be used by God as part of God's sovereign plan to position Joseph for His purposes, even from unlikely places, like the dungeons of an Egyptian prison.

How do I feel when bad things happen to me?

Sometimes, it is helpful to take a step back. By looking at things from a different perspective can really change the way we perceive God's hand in a situation.

I found a picture of a vehicle accident. It happened just outside Flagstaff, Arizona on U.S. Hwy 100 vi. The driver and his passenger are standing by their ute.

When we zoom out, we can see where the driver has broken through the guard-rail, on the right side of the culvert. There are people there, standing on the road, pointing.

The ute was travelling about 75mph from right to left when it crashed through the guard-rail. It flipped end-over-end bounced off and across the culvert outlet, and landed right side up on the left side of the culvert, facing the opposite direction from which the driver was travelling. The 22-year-

old driver and his 18-year-old passenger were unhurt except for minor cuts and bruises.

An accident is not a positive thing... it is a trough experience. I understand that. But, by taking a step back, to look at things from a different perspective, a different angle, can provide us with the sense, that God is present, even in the troughs. Sometimes in miraculous ways.

When have a taken a step back and looked at things from God's perspective? What changes?

God is always present in both the ridge experiences and the trough moments, not one more than the other. God is present in both places, helping us, positioning us, empowering us to keep going.

To acknowledge that God is with us in the trough of suffering, can be challenging. But it is an important affirmation to note we are trusting God even in the difficult places. It is by God's strength that we are continuing to do well with what he has given us, either on the ridge or in the trough. This is an important challenge that Joseph models of us: doing life with God, regardless of whether it is a ridge or a trough.

Prayer:

Thank you, Father God, that the blessing you pour into our lives is from experiencing your presence. Thank you that even in the low points that you carry the presence of God with us. Help us to be channels of blessing to others, even in those low places. Help us carry light into dark places, and care into a world that doesn't care less. Thank you that it is by your Spirit that we are able to do these things.
In Jesus Name, Amen.

5.
The Ridge of Service

Where have been...

Joseph has been to the bottom of a deep trough when he is interned in the Egyptian prison. Yet even here he is aware that God is with him and the blessing exists in his awareness of God's presence with us even in a trough of suffering.

Bible Reading
Genesis 41:1-8

Waiting actively: Kept going

The ray of hope that there may be an advocate that had direct access to Pharoah through the cupbearer, is now gone. Another two years have passed. Two more years of life in a revolting dungeon. Yet there is every indication that Joseph does not give up but continues to pray and wait for the salvation of himself from this prison.

Joseph doesn't let himself go. He doesn't despair or curl up in a corner. He continues to keep going. His waiting is active, engaged, purposeful. He gets up every morning and attends to the next lot of prisoners. He keeps going

Kept busy

Joseph kept busy. He continued to steward what God had placed in his hand even in the trough. He continued to serve those who were in his circle of influence, even without recognition, or appreciation, or being remembered. And I think that even if there was no more to this story, that even if Joseph was forever forgotten in that Egyptian prison, then he would still have been a hero of the faith. He still would have pleased God's heart because of his attitude of humble service, passing onto others some of what God had given him. We are privileged to have insight into a different ending of the story but for Joseph he could only see what he was dealing with right now.

How active is my waiting?

Joseph could only hold on by faith, that God had more, because of what his visions had revealed to him. But right now he kept busy. He is actively waiting. Joseph knew and understood that the dream he was given came from God, and the outworking and delivery of those dreams also belonged to God.

At one point I felt the financial pressure to re-enter the workforce after being a stay-at-home-mother for over decade. I remember looking at what was in my hand and feeling very unemployable: I felt skill-less and quite out of my depth for what the current workforce looked like. A lot can change in a decade. Then quite miraculously, I had a series of three jobs, each position lasted for nine months, progressively more demanding than the previous role. God was up-skilling me.
Then I had the opportunity to apply for a permanent role that had me travelling all over Australia, working in a health and safety team. God took me from the trough of unemployment and provided me with a position and the skills that went with it.

Kept the faith

Just because Joseph got on with his life, does not mean that he had given up on the vision God gave him. It does not mean he did not believe God had more. It does not mean that he gave up on the conviction that this trough would not last forever. He kept the faith.

He stood on his faith in the sure conviction that God was doing what was needed to move him to the next thing, when the time was right. We know that God is already doing stuff in the background. Some of it was seen and some of it was unseen. God is moving and positioning in supernatural ways.

Then after two years Pharoah has two dreams. And just like the dreams of the cupbearer and the baker, Pharoah knows that these dreams are a supernatural messenger to him. They are explicit in their detail and because Pharoah was in a position of privilege and power, he had access to all the priests, and magi and wisemen and magicians in all of his empire. Not one of them could give a definite response about what this dream could really be about. These dreams are a disturbing mystery to them all.

Bible Reading
Genesis 41:9-16

The Waiting is over: Suddenly!

Suddenly Joseph is dragged out his trough of suffering and waiting is over! Suddenly he is thrown into an urgent wardrobe makeover, so he is presentable to the king. Suddenly everything shifts.

If Joseph had to worry about preparing in ways that were more than just a shave and a change of clothes, this moment would have been lost. But he had been preparing for this moment for many, many years. The *'suddenly'* didn't throw him.

Set and Ready

Do you like how Pharoah cuts to the chase? No preamble. Just tell me the meaning of my dream. The *suddenly* didn't throw Joseph because his *head* was in the right space and his *heart* was in the right space. He had no time to pray up; he had to be already prayed up. He had no time to clear his head; or prepare a speech. It was lights, camera, action. He was on. Now! Ready – Set – Go! His *head* was in the right space because he had been actively, faithfully believing for this all along. His *heart* was in the right space because he was actively aware of God's presence with him all along.

Am I prepared for the "suddenly"? Am I all prayed up? Is my head and my heart in the best possible place before God?

This situation has echoes of a parable Jesus told about the groom coming suddenly and some of the bride's attendants were ready and prepared, their lamps were trimmed and filled with oil and some of the were not prepared.

Bible Reference
Matthew 25:1-13

Joseph has his lamp trimmed and filled with oil. He was ready.

Signpost

Joseph gets his audience with Pharoah. He does not plead against his charges or the injustice, He is not pandering for political favour. Joseph is not procuring religious position to add his dream interpretations to another wise man in the empire. He is not afraid of disfavour from the king, who on a whim impales the baker. Joseph stands confidently before the Pharoah of Egypt whose entire subjects believed he was god-incarnate: god in the form of a man. There were many Egyptian gods that Pharoah was to embody.

> The sun god – Ra... who they attribute created the world and who burns to destroy;
> The cobra goddess Wadjet;
> The hawk god Horus;
> The vulture goddess Nekhbet.

Joseph doesn't pretend to be more than he is. The first words that Joseph speaks after being a slave for thirteen years, and in a prison for a good portion of that time is, "I can't do what you ask."

Bible Reference
Genesis 41:16

"But... God will!" God Elôhìym, the living God; the supreme God; The true creator God. God Elôhìym will do what you desire. Here we have a man, humbled by the troughs of his life, standing before the Emperor of Egypt, holding himself with great dignity, great confidence, great discernment, even after he has been suddenly and unexpectedly dragged from his low trough of suffering and waiting. And his first words are as a *signpost* to a greater power, a greater order, a greater deity.

Am I a signpost to God? Or am I quick to point to someone else... or even myself?

Subtly his message is – "You are not god, obviously, or you would know the meaning of your dream. However, God, the true God, the living God, Does have the ability to do this impossible request.

God is not mad at you. God is for you. God has given you the dream and he will likewise give you the answer to your questions; the answer to your confusion; the answer to your fear.'

Joseph is also humbly delivering another message: "I am not mad at you; or the injustice of my suffering; I am willing to be used by God to serve you. I will be the signpost to God in this."

Bible Reading
Genesis 41: 28-44

Rise to the Occupying Ridge

Sometimes, I have read the story of Joseph, and focused significantly on his rise to pre-eminence. Now he is appointed to a position of power. Now he carries on his hand the ring of authority. Now his word carries the full force of the army of Egypt behind him. That means Potiphar – the captain of the guard, who threw him in prison, is now at his beck and call.

But now for me, there is a very big *'but'* in this emphasis. This applauds on Joseph on the ridge and assumes that Joseph on the ridge is successful but implies that Joseph in the trough there was failure. This assumes that the trough was wrong, and the Ridge is righting that wrong.

But it was God's faithfulness in the trough that made the rise to the ridge possible.
But it was Joseph's faithfulness in the trough that made occupying the ridge possible.

But it was God's grace and his divine purposes that were much bigger than one man's prosperity on a ridge that God was inviting Joseph to be part of, by occupying the ridge.

If occupying the ridge becomes about getting back what we deserve, then I think we miss a great divine invitation that we are offered in this story.

Regulate and Reserve

Joseph speaks with great discernment. Good years are coming, and they will be quickly swallowed up by the suffering that is following.

Regulate and reserve now. Regulate resources now for what is coming. Reserve the abundance now for the lean that will follow. Prepare now, for then. Hold in store now for later.

We see another form of ridge and trough – plenty and famine. Have you ever wondered why God didn't give Jacob the heads up about this pending disaster? Israel, as his name is now, is the patriarch of God's chosen family, why didn't he give Israel this word of knowledge? They were spiritual people – they knew the God of Abraham, Isaac and Jacob. They were people of means, this was a prosperous family. They could have activated a similar strategy of regulation and reserve if they had known, at least sufficiently to preserve their family.

Yet God gives this prophetic information to a Pharoah who would presume to be god in his place. That seems odd, unfair almost, if we don't zoom out, and look at the over-arching narrative of the story of God's people. God has a plan, a plan of salvation that is encompassing all people, for eternity, not just a season of seven good years and seven years of famine. His purposes are longer and wider and deeper than that.

Robe of service

God's invitation to Joseph was to be part of those long, wide, deep plans and purposes. And to do this, he offers Joseph another job: to wear the *robe of service*.

How well do I wear the robe of service?

We've seen Joseph's colourful *robe of favoured sonship*, that caused jealousy and triggered betrayal. We've seen the responsible *robe of stewardship*... that was used to frame him. Now Joseph is offered by God, a *robe of service*.

The account records that Pharoah said this, and he did that, yet we know it is God who the sovereign force in this story. God's sovereignty, and his wisdom, is the overarching authority. Joseph becomes the conduit of blessing to those entrusted to his care. This time, on a much larger scale.

Jospeh is appointed Prime Minister – second in charge only to the king. Joseph looks upon this position as a *robe of service*, rather than a robe that puts him up above others, or out in front of others, or over others. I love the way F. B. Meyer puts this:

"At the best, we are but God's almoners, passing on to others the good things, of which God has made us the stewards.
Joseph was set on using all he had, not for himself, but for others."[vii]

"Almoners" is an old-fashioned term referring to those who distribute alms to the poor. This is how Joseph wore the humble robe of service.

Where am I an almoner in the kingdom of God, passing on the good things God has given me to others?

Joseph is given responsibility, and he works hard to steward what has been placed in his hand with integrity. He did that in the trough. He does it again, as the opportunity was offered to him. He occupied this ridge of service and kept the same pattern.

Sometimes positioning occurs quite miraculously. When God started to stimulate my thinking about my involvement in working with his bride – the church, I initially was not on board. As a lay-person I had a firm conviction that we are all called to a life of "ministry" regardless of various roles we might hold. That had always been my mindset, so for me the invitation God was presenting was about engaging more officially within the established church. I had a conversation with one of my pastors and disclosed God was working on my "ambitions" and I thought they were bold and quite audacious. He pushed me to disclose what these were, but given these were only formation ideas at this stay I didn't feel this was appropriate, so I didn't share that. At this stage, it was between me and God.
Ironically because I didn't give voice to these ideas I could immediately see, very transparently, that he was looking at me through his lens of what his 'ambition' looked like, not mine. But now, looking back, I think it is hilarious. I seriously can say that the extent of my ambition and what I was referring to at that time was to work in the "church office". That was it. God was asking me to be more involved in his church and that was all I could picture. I possibly could do the office work. As I started sussing out what might be needed to do this, one lady who worked in the church office looked me over and said to me, "I'm not worried about my job at all. You would never get this job."

Yet God didn't argue, but he held ambitions for me that were far more than I could see. He positioned and trained and maneuvered on my behalf to have me appointed in a role of being a shepherd and pastor, that was over and above what I could ever conceive. God did this. Not me. That was his positioning so that I can be one of God's many almoners, passing on to others the good things, which God has made us the stewards over. God is inviting us to occupy the opportunities he has given us whether on the ridge or in the trough, "not for ourselves, but for others..."

Joseph now occupies a high, high ridge which is God's positioning, not his. Even here, God's presence goes with him. Joseph is not like the cupbearer, who forgets God's kindness to him, but carries that with him as he discharges his responsibilities before him.

Some final thoughts...

Joseph actively engaged in his low troughs, so that he was ready for the 'suddenly'. Here, he is invited to occupy a very high ridge of service. Joseph gets on with stewarding his responsibilities consistently, with integrity, and dignity. He is positioned in a place of influence in miraculous ways. Joseph doesn't forget that even in this high place, God is with him. The blessing is in the *presence* of God not just in the ridge of influence and success.

Prayer:

Father God, we thank you that you do gift us with many good things in our lives. Today, Father, whether we are experiencing a trough, or occupying a ridge, that we would be able to be 'almoners' of your love, and your grace, and your resources to pass them on to those around us. Help us to see where you would have us do this.
In Jesus Name, Amen.

6.

The Trough of Suspicion

Where we are up to...

Joseph is appointed by Pharoah as Governor of Egypt, and he has a very public and influential life. However, just because he is now a public figure, that doesn't mean he is exempt from the experience of troughs. Sometimes these experiences can be very private places, unseen by those around us.

I had an opportunity to talk with some ladies in a remote PNG village. I wondered how I could connect with them and not present as some white woman coming in on the outside. What chose to share was about something that was very close to my heart during that time: our private battles, our private tears, the things that no one sees, and therefore no one acknowledges, even the things we find hard to talk about. What surprised me was the resonance and the connection of hearts that we experienced in at village hut with a thatched roof and bamboo slatted floor. This wasn't an isolated personal experience; it wasn't a cultural experience to the exclusion of others; this is a human experience that crosses the lines of family, and community and culture. Some troughs we go through are private, and unseen for many reasons.

Have I ever experienced a hidden struggle, a private trough experience that others were not aware of?

How can I build stronger trustworthy relationships that can share my very raw and honest moments?

Bible Reading
Genesis 42: 1-28

Confronting our past in the present

In this story we are given insight into a hidden struggle that Joseph encounters, a private trough he is dealing with which is unknown and unseen by those around him.

Time has been marching on. Seven good years have been, and the seven years of famine are underway. This means that Joseph is now about 40 years old. He looks like an Egyptian. He speaks Egyptian. His name is Egyptian. His wife is Egyptian. He is immersed in his work as Governor or Egypt, administrating the affairs of the Egyptian Kingdom. Everything about his life is Egyptian on the outside.

The famine is harsh and widespread, and early on in the first couple of years, Jacob sends his sons to Egypt to buy supplies.

Bible Reference
Genesis 45:6

Suddenly Joseph is confronted by his past, in his very Egyptian looking present. Suddenly he is confronted by the things that brought him to this place. Suddenly he is confronted by a trough on the inside that is just as real as the slavery he experienced and the prison he lived in.

Sometimes our troughs are private matters, unseen and unrecognisable to those around us. They are troughs none the less. Joseph recognises his brothers, lined up in the queue to buy rations, the same men who sold him into slavery 25 years later.

Informed by the past

These are the same men who betrayed him. The same men who were deaf to his pleas for mercy. The same men who threw him in a hole, and who plotted his death of revenge while he listened. The same men who despised his relationship with his beloved father. These men, full of hate, bent on revenge, are here now, bowing down to him.

Suddenly Joseph has a flash back! Dreams of wheat sheaves bowing down; the sun and the moon bowing down. Joseph knew and understood that the dream he was given came from God, and in that moment, he was witnessing the outworking and delivery of those dreams in what was happening right before his eyes.

There is a common lore saying that I often hear: "We can't look back to the past, we should only move forward." I would suggest that our past informs our present. Everything we experience, every choice that we make, every action of others, in some way informs our present and what is happening now.

Do I think more of the past, present or future? What is a balance way to hold these parts of our life?

We don't come to our present in a vacuum. Rather we come to 'now', impacted and informed, by what has brought us here to this moment. Our past informs our present, but it doesn't mean we try to stay in a static state of what the past used to look like. Rather, our past informs our present. It doesn't dictate what happens now, but we can use our learnings to feed into the choices that we make from this time forward.

What is it like to think that my experiences from my past can inform my present, but they don't need to dictate what I do?

Investigating intent

Joseph's wisdom is that in begins a process of investigating what is going on here. Rather than dive in with revenge, or payback, or even premature reconciliation, he pauses and buys himself time. At first glance, his harsh treatment of his brothers, could be seen as vengeful and vindictive, but there is something else going on here.

I believe Joseph is actually investigating whether these people, who did him great harm, have changed. Are they the same men, with the same agendas, just standing now in a different setting, or a different context? He hasn't seen his brothers for twenty-five years. He doesn't know what has happened to them between then and now. There is more to be learned.

Bible Reading
Genesis 42: 15-38

Testing Trust versus Disloyalty

I notice is that Joseph's tears are unseen by others. This is painful, but in this moment, there is no one apart from God who shares this pain. Joseph proceeds to put in place things that would occur that would bring his brothers, father and Benjamin back to him.

He hears their conversation in Hebrew, and already his brothers are connecting dots that relate to the consequences of how they treated Joseph so long ago. They see that their past choices are in some way, impacting the present. Reuben accuses the others of not being dependable, lack of respect, lack of regard and not listening. They are still not sounding loyal to their family or to each other.

Perhaps not much has changed after all.

Deceit and Violence

Joseph takes Simeon and interns him in prison as surety, until they make a decision to return to verify the story of their circumstances.

Why Simeon?

Simeon the second eldest son in the family – born to Leah. I have assumed this was a random choice, however there are some traditions around why Simeon might have been singled out for this 'privilege'.

There is an account in Genesis 34, before Joseph was born, where Simeon and Levi violently avenge their sister Dinah after she was defiled by the son of an influential man from the community of Shechem near where Jacob had settled their family. These two brothers deceitfully pretended to be open to a treaty of peace. Part of their terms of this man marrying Dinah, was that they expected the men of the city to be circumcised for religious reasons, before the alliance could be enacted.

The community agreed, and then two days later while all the men were very sore and unable to move or defend themselves, Simeon and Levi come in and slaughter all the males of the community. Wholesale slaughter. Then the whole community was looted, they carried off the women to serve in their households, and livestock was stolen to pad their herds. This was an act of war.

Their father, Jacob, knew nothing of it until it was done, but now he had to deal with the fallout. Jacob said, his family was now a stench, a stink, a bad smell, odious to their neighbours.

Bible Reference
Genesis 34:30

This speaks to the style of Simeon and Levi. Deceit. Violence. Bullying. Acting on rage, rather than with self-control. Hebrew tradition suggests that Simeon was one of the main players in Joseph's abduction when he was seventeen years old and was the one who initiated the threats to kill him and was saved by Judah's alternate plan of selling him as a slave.

Regardless, Simeon is separated out, and detained in prison, while the others go back to their father Jacob, with Joseph's proposal and conditions if they want more supplies of grain from Egypt.

When I think about people who have perpetrated problems in my past, am I quick for revenge? Am I quick to re-engage?

Do I show caution, to discern what is really going on?

Devotion

Joseph has a great concern for his father. He has carried great affection for his father all these years. His brothers previously totally disregarded his father's feelings. Was there evidence that this had changed? Are his brothers genuinely concerned for their father now? Joseph also holds a great affection for his brother Benjamin also. So underpinning Joseph's harsh words, his abrupt accusations, he is the testing the water of their devotion, their regard, and looking for evidence that things have changed.

Directs a refund

Then Joseph does something that doesn't seem like a test but is often interpreted as such. He commands a refund of the brother's money to be secretly put into the brother's sacks. How would his brother's respond to this act? Would they honestly disclose their money had been returned? I like the idea that Joseph was demonstrating his own freedom from everything in the past which had kept him a slave. Mindsets have been shifted from what had kept him bound. He was sold for silver but now he is able to generously act in the *opposite spirit* by offering silver as a gift. He had been betrayed, but he could now be openhanded. His brothers had bound him, but he could release them with an opportunity to *be* better and *do* better. They had been deaf to his suffering, but he had listened to their plight and supported their journey home.

Is there some matter which has kept me bound which I need to release by acting in the opposite spirit?

Bible Reading
Genesis 43: 1-3; 15-34

This is the brothers' second trip to Egypt. We see more of Joseph's cautious engagement with his brothers. On the surface he is authoritarian, and brash. But there is more going on.

Protective

They return with Benjamin – his younger brother. I've had it in my mind that Benjamin is still a youth, but it is more likely he is now a man in his 30s. Still his father is defensive of him and does not want to let him go. Jacob had released Joseph to conduct family business once and he never saw him again.

Reuben and Judah offer surety for Benjamin and finally Jacob consents to allow the brothers to return to Egypt.

Bible Reference
Genesis 42:37; 43:9

So, the brothers arrive in Egypt and Benjamin is with them. The decision to return is catapulted by the desperate need for food. I think there is wisdom in Joseph's cautious re-engagement with these men. Some interpret his approach as payback. What I see, is a cautious checking of their circumstances and nature.

Pledge & Payment

Desperation has Jacob release Benjamin to go to Egypt, only with Judah's commitment of surety for his safety. There is a sincerity in their commitment that we haven't seen before. They put their own families on the line to demonstrate their commitment to Benjamin's safety. What we see, is a sincere attempt to make restitution. They collaborated in something that was not right before but this time – they are doing it differently.

When their payment for their grain was found in the mouth of their grain sacks, they didn't just celebrate their good luck, they are distressed and suspicious. So, they brought the return payment, plus additional money for their new supplies. This is a big deviation from their previous attitudes.

They even follow up with Joseph's steward, about the error and their desire to make restitution

Private trough

Joseph dines with his brothers, but still there is a mask of cautious conventions around their visit. Joseph asks after their father's health. He meets his brother Benjamin after 25 years.

I like the picture of him seating his brothers according to their age, and their astonishment as they realise, they have been seated according to age. Reuben, Simeon, Levi, Judah right down to Benjamin. Yet Joseph still stands behind the Egyptian protocols that he adheres to. They ate at different tables. It says Hebrews were detestable to the Egyptians. They were foreigners. They were sheepherders.

Remember, the Hebrews are not a nation at this time. This is just a small tribal family from Canaan, influential in their own region. There is no Law of Moses binding them together. They have no scripture or law books. They just have a verbal history of their family of Terah, Abraham, Isaac and Jacob. Have no doubt: this family is insignificant in the eyes of the world power of the Egyptians. Yet they are not insignificant in the eyes of God.

As Joseph re-engages with his brothers, he is overwhelmed by this encounter. He removes himself to gather and regulate and settle. These people are his family! Regardless of the history of pain, and betrayal, he is noticing a change. Joseph's suspicions are nearly resolved but as yet, he is not completely convinced. He vigilantly holds himself apart.

This trough is a private experience. His boss doesn't know. His subjects don't know. Most likely his wife and family doesn't know. His brothers are completely confused as to what is happening. Just him and God. And yet just like the troughs that were public and known, God is with him in this private experience as well.

How can I build relationships that are strong in the good years so we have access to them in the lean years?

Some final thoughts...

On the outside Joseph is occupying a ridge. He is the governor or prime minister of Egypt, holding a most influential position of the reigning world power. Yet in this story Joseph experiences a private trough, so private, that those around him would not be aware of what is happening for him. Joseph is confronted with his past, and it is a difficult thing. He sees in person the vision that God had given him 25 years ago. But he is also aware of the betrayal and pain inflicted at their hand. He is on a journey of forgiveness and restoration.

I have included some steps towards forgiveness in the Appendix 'Offering and Seeking Forgiveness' at the end of this book, which may be helpful to consider if this is a trough you are experiencing. Whether this is a private trough that happens under the radar, or something others are aware of, forgiveness is always personal, and it isn't easy.

Prayer:

Thank you, Father God that you walk with us through the dark valleys, and through the trough-times, regardless of whether other people see or recognise our journey. Thank you that your plan is for us to do life in family, and we ask Holy Spirit that you would help us to work to be more aligned with your model of family, not of jealousy, vindictiveness, revenge and payback. Help us to forgive where forgiveness is needed and to go slowly protecting boundaries where that is also needed. Help us through love, grace and mercy that we would show discernment and compassion.
In Jesus name, Amen.

7.

The Ridge of Sonship

Where we are up to...

Joseph is prime minister of the Egyptian empire. He is a man of incredible power and influence at the positioning of God. And into that ridge experience he was plunged into a private trough as he is confronted with his past. His brothers came to Egypt to purchase food to survive the famine.

As a child I remember a project that my grandfather was undertaking to record our family story. Some of it was historical and some of it was a snapshot in time of a contribution that we could all make. Grandpa asked me to play a piece on the piano for this project. He had a brand-new cassette recorder and with this astounding modern technology he was recording our family story. I so wanted to do this well! Really well. But I had a problem. As a child I was incredibly nervous and physically shake and turn to jelly in front of people.
But, being a child of faith, I prayed and asked God to make the impossible happen and take away my 'nerves' so I could do this for Grandpa. I believed it whole heartedly. So, when I was given the nod to start, I started to play. And it was terrible! I crashed through that item and mutilated that piece of music from beginning to end.
But, being a child of faith, I believed that perhaps God could take that musical mess and, in some magical way, make it sound as good as I had

> *hoped. So, I waited to hear what it sounded like. My meticulous Grandfather was frowning, and crawling in behind the piano, and checking the cords, when he eventually coughed embarrassed and said, "Olwyn, honey, I am so sorry, but I forgot to plug it in. Would you mind terribly to play it again?"*
>
> *My heart leapt because I knew God had answered my prayer! I had another opportunity and this time, I played it flawlessly!*
>
> *I have wondered why God didn't do that the first time. Why go through the humiliation of that first failure? But I think I would not have that experience of how God can take a mess and transform it in unexpected ways. Not by magic, but as a journey of being together in the trough to see something good emerge.*

Sometimes we want God to use 'magic' and take an impossible problem and magically transform it into our ideal circumstances. The invitation in the story of Joseph for us, is to remember that God is with us in all circumstances, that our blessing exists in our awareness of the presence of God in our lives, in either ridge or trough experiences. But although God does not use magic, he is still working circumstances towards our good.

Where can I see that God has turned something bad, a trough experience, into something good?

As we conclude our reflections on the life of Joseph and his story is one that ends on a ridge experience. Let's read where Joseph has worked through his private challenges and now reveals himself to his brothers.

Bible Reading
Genesis 45: 1-9

Sent ahead to Protect lives

This is the story of a great reveal. Joseph reveals himself to his brothers. He sends away his attendants, and the other officials who were sharing this meal, and he is left alone with his brothers. Although this is something that he does as private audience with his brothers, the matter is so emotional that his whole household heard about it. The household of Pharaoh heard about it. Something quite remarkable is happening here. Joseph has worked through his trough of suspicion. He forgives the treachery and the betrayal and looks at a bigger picture, God's sovereignty in this situation.

Three times he boldly declares "God sent me ahead of you." He has been given insight into God's purposes here.
Regardless of their bad behaviour.
Regardless of their malicious intent.
Regardless of their issues and their lack of character.
God was overwriting their weakness with his purposes and sovereignty.

In chapter 41 – it is recorded where Pharaoh gave Joseph a new Egyptian name

Bible Reference
Genesis 41:45

Joseph has new name – Zaphenath-Paneah which means *"one who discovers hidden things"*. Another meaning may have been *"preserver of the age"*. Joseph not only uncovers the hidden meaning of dreams, but he was able to discern the hidden matters of the kingdom of God. Joseph doesn't just see himself as an employee or subject of Egypt, but first as an employee and subject of the Kingdom of God. God sent him. His role, as his name suggests was to be the preserver of the age. To save lives; to protect lives; to alleviate suffering. Joseph is a type or a pattern of a redeemer here, a saviour, one who saves and preserves through the purposes and pattern of God's grace.

Sent ahead to Preserve a Remnant

Joseph was given influence and position – not for his own comfort and vindication, but for the purpose to preserve a remnant. A portion. A residual part. Joseph zooms out, and understands, his positioning was not just about Egypt. He was commissioned and positioned by God. He was not the victim of his brothers' malicious intent. As a subject of the Kingdom of God – it holds the higher order & purpose. This was not about the reigning world power, and the known kingdoms of civilisation at this time, but it was actually about his own family: God's chosen family of Israel.

This *was* about his own insignificant family – those who were despised by the Egyptians. *They* were to be preserved.

This *was* also about his dreams. They were messages of comfort pointing to God's purposes. Confirmation that God is the prevailing master of grace.

This *was* about his father and his brothers and their families. He was positioned to preserve those who had turned against him. In a famine – a famine that was so far and wide and destructive, Joseph was sent ahead, 25 years ahead, to preserve, for God, a remnant for God's purposes.

Sent ahead to Perform a great Deliverance

Joseph speaks of a great deliverance. Yes. it included his immediate family, but it is also bigger than that. This was not *just* about his own family. Here we see the layering of God's purposes. This seven-year deliverance from famine, was the forerunner of God's great deliverance.

Where do I need God to perform a great deliverance?

This is bigger than Joseph's family. This is bigger than Egypt where Joseph is presiding as governor. This is bigger than the known world at this time. God is fixing to perform a *great* deliverance, through the family of Abraham, Isaac and Jacob. This is a prophetic declaration, into even the greater purposes of God. Did Joseph understand the extent of his declaration? Probably not.

Did Joseph understand the magnificent scope of what God is doing, in terms of spiritual salvation, not just alleviating human starvation in 1706 BC? Probably not.

Did he understand the promise made to his great-grandfather, Abraham, that through his family, all humanity will be blessed? Perhaps, in part.

Bible Reference
Genesis 18:18; 22:18; 26:4

The prophetic voice of Joseph is reinforcing that God is bigger. God is grander. God is stronger. God is the mastermind of purposes that encompass the engineering of a great deliverance!

Bible Reading
Genesis 47: 1-30

Reunited

There is a drawing together of various threads in this story. He is reunited with Benjamin – his full-blood brother. He unveils his identity to his half-brothers. He allows for the possibility that he would see his aged father alive, after all these years.

Joseph brings his entire family back to Egypt so that they can survive the remaining five years of severe famine. Joseph is reunited with his father. I think there is beautiful symmetry in that Jacob lives with Joseph in Egypt for seventeen years.

Seventeen years. Jacob had seventeen years with Joseph as he was growing up. And now Jacob has that same amount of time as he is reunited with his lost son. In many ways it would have been like a resurrection for Jacob as he realised that Joseph was really alive.

Resourced

There is no doubt in Joseph's mind that what God has revealed to him will come to pass. Two years of the famine have passed and already the people from all around are travelling to Egypt to buy grain just to survive. Egypt is usually associated with oppression and slavery, however, here we see it as a God-ordained place of refuge.

There are a few notable times where this is idea of Egypt as a place of 'refuge' is seen in the biblical accounts:

Abraham went there to survive a famine
Bible Reference:
Genesis 12:10-20

Joseph and Mary went there with the child Jesus to escape the hand of Herod.
Bible Reference:
Matthew 2:13-14

Jacob's entire family (seventy in all) went there to survive a famine.
Bible Reference:
Genesis 46:6

We know that God has positioned Joseph to resource his family through this devastating famine. He settles them in the best land that Egypt has to offer: the region of Goshen. Goshen is at the southern end of the Nile delta. It is fertile. It has water. It is an oasis in a widespread and devastating drought and famine.

Joseph is the administrator for all the grain distribution. He can assure that Jacobs' family is not left out, because of their 'despicable' profession or being foreigners. They get an allocated share.

Reconciliation

As the world is under the oppression of a horrible natural disaster, there is a beautiful reconciliation that is happening in this family.

Bible Reading
Genesis 47:19-21; 48:11-22; 50:15-21
Even though there is a famine ravaging the known world, the story of Joseph finishes on a ridge. Joseph is restored back into his birth family. He is given a place that becomes more meaningful for him, than the prestige and position as the governor of Egypt.

He is, ironically, gifted a parcel of land from Jacob, as his inheritance, that geographically is a ridge. It is land that Jacob had secured by his own hand.

What is it like to think that God bestows on me the reconciliation of sonship?

Betrayal and abandonment are taken away, and it is replaced with blessing and sonship. Joseph's position in the family is legitimised. Joseph's own sons, Ephraim and Manasseh, are given legitimacy into the house of Israel. Even though Judah takes on the role of the first-born, (after Reuben, Simeon and Levi are disqualified) the adoption of Ephraim and Manasseh, means that Joseph has also been allocated that "double portion" of the first born. Joseph is now occupying another ridge, the ridge of sonship.

But after Jacob dies, Joseph's brothers become very fearful of their own vulnerable position. They understand the depth of their depravity and that now it is possible that Joseph is in the position where he could hold them to account for those actions. They again prostrate themselves and bow low before Joseph. They declare that they would be willing to serve Joseph as his slaves. That is a curious declaration.

All of Egypt has been progressively being drawn into the bondage of slavery as the famine progresses at Joseph's initiative. If people could not pay for food because they had no money left, they sold their livestock to Pharoah. If they had no livestock left, they sold their land and property to Pharoah. If they had no land left, then they sold themselves and were bonded in slavery to Pharaoh, to save their lives.

Joseph's brothers come voluntarily to him with the same proposal. "Yes," they said, "they would be Joseph's slaves." Yet Joseph says "*No!*" He would not reduce his father's family to slaves, even though Joseph willingly enforced the whole nation of Egypt into servitude to Pharoah without pause.

Am I quick to offer myself into slavery to get out of a problem?

So, it would seem, that by the end of this seven-year famine, the nation of Egypt are bonded as slaves to Pharoah as their monarch. Other peoples and tribes who came looking for food are bonded to Pharoah as the ruling world power. And yet, the family of Israel, are given an exemption from this edict.

The way I read this is that the family and people of Israel are the only free people in this land. We know this is not always the case, but right now, even though it looks like a famine, God is positioning his people to flourish. Joseph makes a beautiful declaration of his God's intent. "*You intended to get rid of me, but God intended to position me for good, to accomplish what is now being done, the saving of many lives.*"

Bible Reference

Genesis 50:20

What sort of "good" can God do through me where I am positioned?

God's intention towards us is always love, always good. Regardless of the troughs that Joseph had to navigate to get there, he can now look back over his life and say: Yes! The goodness of God has followed me! God intended it for good!

It is on this note that Genesis, the book of beginnings concludes:
God is faithful.
God is faithful to be with us, through the troughs and the ridges.
God is faithful, regardless of our mistakes and our issues.
God is faithful and his presence goes with us, to turn harm into good, betrayal into blessing, devastation into salvation.

Some final thoughts...

As the story of Joseph concludes, we find he is occupying a ridge. He is reunited with his family, reconciled with his brothers and restored to his beloved father.

Joseph acknowledges he has been resourced to accomplish a great deliverance. This is a ridge experience of forgiveness, reconciliation, and restoration. It is the ridge of sonship, even though on the outside, all those around him can only see famine, and hardship, and slavery.

> *An Amish father and son went on an excursion to the outside world, to the big city. They were amazed at the tall buildings, and the fast cars, and the danger at every turn. They went inside one of the big buildings and stood amazed as they witnessed the most incredible phenomenon. There in front of them were magic doors.*
> *They watched gobsmacked as people walked through these magic doors and when they opened them again, they had disappeared.*
> *Lots of people would walk into the doors and the doors would silently close and then as they waited only a couple of people would walk out.*
> *Then a man came with an elderly woman, crippled in a wheelchair – the doors opened and in they went, the doors closed.*
> *They waited and sure enough the doors opened and out stepped a beautiful young woman. The father turned to his son flabbergasted, and said, "Quick Ezra go and get your mother!"*

God did not use magic doors in Joseph's life. God didn't make betrayal, and prison, and suspicion go away, he had to live through those trough experiences, day by day, year by year. Still, he was aware that God was with him in those places, and Joseph became a conduit of blessing in those places. When he could not see, he trusted God was working in the mess and with the mess for good. And then later on, he could see how good that 'good' God was working on!

Right at the beginning of this series I came with the question: Should I fight the troughs? Should I try and navigate life, in such a way that I only stay positioned on a ridge? Or does the landscape of our lives, naturally fall into a natural profile of troughs and ridges?

What has this story helped us understand about our own experiences of ridges and troughs?

What is it like to remind myself, God is with me... in the troughs and on the ridges?

I think, I take comfort from the idea that life is naturally full of ups and downs. I also take comfort from the idea, that regardless of what it looks like on the outside, God is with us, God *intends that* what we face is for good, our good and he can, and will turn it around. Here are some promises to reflect on.

Bible Reference
2 Corinthians 9:8
Romans 8:28

God is inviting us to be aware of his presence with us in all things, at all times, whether in the trough or on the ridge. That is the abundant blessing of his promise to us. He is with us!

Prayer:

Father God, we thank you that you are so remarkable. We thank you for your sovereignty. We thank you for your presence in our lives. We thank you that you are with us in the trough and work to transform us to be people who can occupy the ridge with integrity. We thank you that You are with us in the trough and on the ridge, You are with us. Regardless of whether it is an Up or a Down Your presence is a constant. Help us to be more aware of you... because this is the place of blessing. Thank you for the declaration that Joseph made, that you are fixing to make a great deliverance. Thank you that we have the privilege of experiencing that great deliverance through Jesus. Thank you that you continue to work in us and through us to continue to transform and change things for our good.
In Jesus name Amen.

Appendix: Offering and Seeking Forgiveness
A-B-C-D-E of offering Forgiveness

A: Offering Forgiveness is an **Act of will**

We activate forgiveness as an intentional choice – consciously, deliberately.

It is a choice that we make despite feelings of hurt and pain and injustice, and abuse, and wrong, and exploitation.

B: Offering Forgiveness is letting go of **Blame**

It is relinquishing resentment, negativity and bitterness.

It is working towards wholeness instead of brokenness, offering kindness instead of cruelty.

It is desiring good things will be experienced instead of bad things.

C: Offering Forgiveness releases **Condemnation**

This is not about letting the other person off the hook – it is acknowledging that being judge and jury is not our role, or place.

Appropriate legal systems can take their course, but it is not our place to take revenge and demand pay-back.

D: Offering Forgiveness is *not* **Denying the pain**

Forgiveness is not ignoring the pain; or pretending there is no hurt. If there is no problem, there is no need for forgiveness. Acknowledging how the issue caused us pain, actually brings clarity and definition to the forgiveness we are offering.

E: Offering Forgiveness includes **Expressing needs & boundaries**

Part of the healing of forgiveness is expressing what are my needs, and what are my expectations around appropriate behaviour in the future.

Note: Forgiveness does not automatically mean reconciliation. Clear boundaries may be needed to ensure emotional or physical safety.

A-B-C-D-E of seeking Forgiveness

A: Seeking Forgiveness is an **Act of will**

We seek forgiveness from someone we have hurt as an intentional choice – consciously, deliberately

It is a choice that we make, to admit what happened was wrong or hurtful, despite feelings of shame or embarrassment; fear or guilt over the situation that has occurred.

B: Seeking Forgiveness is not attributing **Blame**

It is being accountable for our contribution to the situation.

This is done without placing blame, or avoiding taking responsibility.

Eliminate the "BUTs"... that will try to rationalise what happened.

C: Seeking Forgiveness Considers **Compensation**

If there is restitution that needs to be made in some way, we do what we can to make this up: repair, restore or replace.

D: Seeking Forgiveness will **Describe our intent to change**

Assure the other person that you will not do it again.

Describe the tangible steps you have in place to change, or to do things differently.

E: Seeking Forgiveness includes Expressing **Empathy**

Part of seeking forgiveness is to express and acknowledging the pain that has been caused by our actions,

Try to understand and recognise the other person's experience of this situation.

Note: Sometimes we can genuinely seek forgiveness, with remorse and genuine intent for reconciliation, but the other person is not able to receive that for various reasons. We cannot make this happen. We do our part gently and know that God forgives us and He will help us to live with more integrity going forward.

Other books in this Series

Endnotes

[i] https://biblehub.com/topical/p/primogeniture.htm

[ii] https://www.gotquestions.org/firstborn-in-the-Bible.html
https://reformjudaism.org/learning/torah-study/torah-commentary/why-firstborns-are-such-big-deal-torah

[iii] Effrey M. Cohen, Early Traditions On The Kidnapping And Sale Of Joseph;
https://jbqnew.jewishbible.org/assets/Uploads/383/saleofjosephpart2.pdf

[iv] Dr. Claude Mariottini – Professor of Old Testament, How Can Someone Sell His Own Brother to the Egyptians?
https://claudemariottini.com/2021/05/24/how-can-someone-sell-his-own-brother-to-the-egyptians/

[v] Dr John Warlow is a psychiatrist based in Brisbane, who works with people to integrate Biblical truth for life transformation. Dr Warlow has published a number of books including 'Living Wholeness: The Christian Wholeness Framework for Professional Counsellors'.

[vi] I have not been able to verify conclusively whether this event actually happened; some of the posts of this situation is dated around 2007. Even if the photo is generated it offers a take on perspective that is an opportunity for reflection.
Downloaded from parentInfluence.com 24/9/2025; People-share-their-lucky-moments-on-social-media by Kristen Reed.

[vii] F. B Meyer commentary for Genesis 41:14-36

www.ingramcontent.com/pod-product-compliance
Lightning Source LLC
Chambersburg PA
CBHW052108070526
44584CB00017B/2389